10/1/13

For Caroline, Jack Brodie, Hayden, Gavin, Sam, and Brian—and with special thanks
to Robbie for his helpful feedback, enthusiasm and baseball expertise —J.W.

To my family —T.W.

AUTHOR'S NOTE

William Howard Mays Jr. was born near Birmingham, Alabama, in the suburb of Westfield, on May 6, 1931.
He began his baseball career when he was only a teen, in 1947, in the Negro Leagues—first with the
Chattanooga Choo-Choos and then with his hometown pennant-winning Birmingham Black Barons. He went
on to become a man who many say was the greatest all-around player in major league history. At the time of
this book's publication, many of Mays's career stats are at or near the top of practically every major league
all-time list. Many seasons he led the league in batting average, homers, stolen bases, triples, runs, hits,
walks, total bases, on-base percentage, slugging percentage, and other categories. Had he not been drafted
into the army, there's a good chance that he would have hit more home runs than even Babe Ruth, whose
714 (the record until 1974) were only 54 more than Mays's 660.

In his quiet way, Willie Mays did much to further the cause of justice for African Americans. He arrived on
the public stage at a time when many white Americans truly thought that African Americans were inferior—
and he proved that this was absolutely ridiculous. He may not have marched in any civil rights parades, as did
Jackie Robinson, the first African American in the majors. But what Mays did on the baseball field was a BIG
eye-opener for white America. He was not just a great "black" baseball player—he was simply *the* greatest
baseball player most people had ever seen. Period.

Text copyright © 2013 by Jonah Winter
Jacket art and interior illustrations copyright © 2013 by Terry Widener
All rights reserved.
Published in the United States by Schwartz & Wade Books,
an imprint of Random House Children's Books,
a division of Random House, Inc., New York.
Schwartz & Wade Books and the colophon
are trademarks of Random House, Inc.
Visit us on the Web! randomhouse.com/kids
Educators and librarians, for a variety of teaching tools,
visit us at RHTeachersLibrarians.com

Library of Congress Cataloging-in-Publication Data
Winter, Jonah.
You never heard of Willie Mays?! / by Jonah Winter ; illustrations by
Terry Widener.
p. cm.
ISBN 978-0-375-86844-3 (trade) — ISBN 978-0-375-96844-0 (glb)
1. Mays, Willie, 1931– —Juvenile literature.
2. Baseball players—United States—Biography—Juvenile literature.
I. Widener, Terry, ill. II. Title.
GV865.M38 W56 2013
796.357092—dc23 [B] 2011047347

The text of this book is set in News 706 BT.
The illustrations were rendered in acrylic on chipboard.
Book design by Rachael Cole

MANUFACTURED IN CHINA
10 9 8 7 6 5 4 3 2 1
First Edition

About the cover: This lenticular cover was created using a plastic sheet composed of a series of
tightly spaced, curved ridges. Each ridge is a tiny lens, called a lenticule. Terry Widener rendered
three images, which were digitally sliced into strips and printed on this plastic sheet, with one
strip from each image behind each lenticule. The lenses let you see only one set of strips at a time,
creating the illusion of movement as you turn the cover.

YOU NEVER HEARD
OF WILLIE MAYS?!

written by **JONAH WINTER**
illustrated by **TERRY WIDENER**

schwartz & wade books · new york

Y ou never heard of Willie Mays?! THE Willie Mays?! Oh, geez, where to begin? How about . . . Birmingham, Alabama. 1941. A kid with his ear glued to the radio:

"We interrupt this program for an important announcement: Joe DiMaggio has just homered off Red Sox pitcher Dick Newsome, extending his hitting streak to a record-breaking forty-five games!"

As the story goes, a little boy named Willie Mays had himself a hero. Willie told his pop, "I wanna be the next Joe DiMaggio."

JOLTIN' JOE

From roughly 1937 to 1950, Joe DiMaggio was considered THE best player on the New York Yankees and one of the top players in the major leagues. He was known for his mighty home run blasts, wide batting stance, unstoppable baserunning, game-winning hits, and unmatchable grace in center field. And in 1941, his hitting streak of fifty-six games set a record that will probably never be broken. All over America, radio stations would announce each time DiMaggio extended his streak.

Word was, Willie did everything like Joltin'
Joe—the batting stance, the way he ran, the
way he threw.

There was only one problem: the major
leagues didn't allow black guys to play back
then—craziest rule there ever was. So maybe
someday this kid could play on a Negro
League team, but wearin' Yankee pinstripes
was out of the question.

In the Deep South, where Willie lived,
black folks had to drink from different water
fountains and sit at the back of the bus.

WHITES

CO

THE NEGRO LEAGUES

Because the major leagues barred all black players, African
Americans formed their own leagues—the Negro Leagues.
They had their own world series, all-star games, and American
and National Leagues, just like the majors. They even played in
some of the same stadiums. Sometimes they played exhibition
games against the major league teams—and they won more
than they lost. Yep, they were better. And many of their stars
are now in the National Baseball Hall of Fame. It's about time.

Most blacks in Birmingham worked backbreaking jobs in the steel mills—that was all they could get. But Willie's pop had made some decent money playin' center field for a semipro team, and he knew how much you could make if you were *really* good—if you were a pro. That's why he was always coachin' Willie how to hit and how to play center.

By all accounts, though, Willie didn't need too many pointers—he was a *natural.* He was the kid all the other kids wanted on their team—the one who ran a little faster, hit a little farther, played a little harder than anybody else.

And he was the kid everybody liked—who entertained his sisters by throwing dishes up in the air and catchin' 'em, just like they were baseballs and this was the World Series!

He was the kid who played with his pop on the steel mill team, who once outran him for a fly ball, because at age fourteen Willie was already the better player.

And he was the kid who in 1946, at only fifteen years old, got asked to play pro ball in the Negro Leagues with grown men—and he did!

Suddenly, this teenage kid was makin' more money than his pop. And when, the year after that, the major leagues ended their stupid rule barrin' black guys, there was a ray of hope that one day Willie might play in the majors, *like Joe DiMaggio.*

What a wild thing that must've been for young Willie, spendin' his summer vacations playin' for teams like the Birmingham Black Barons, ridin' round the country in a rickety bus through the night 'cause no whites-only hotels would put 'em up, gettin' teased by the older guys, who knew in their hearts he was already better than them, that he was goin' places, even though his voice was still squeaky and his arms were still skinny and he still had a lot to learn.

Legend has it, the first time Willie got hit by a pitch, he was lyin' on the ground, wind knocked out of him, practically cryin'. His coach walks up to him and says, "Son, can you see first base?"

"Y-y-y-yes sir," Willie squeaks.

"Then I want you to get up and walk there. And the first chance you get, I want you to steal second."

Well, as it turned out, Willie did steal second, and third—and scored a run!

And he kept on runnin' and runnin' and runnin' . . .

. . . all the way to the major leagues! It was 1951, and there weren't too many black guys in the majors yet— they had to be mind-bogglingly good to make the cut. The team that signed him was the New York Giants—and for us Giants fans, this was a BIG deal. See, we were just a so-so team back then—we never got higher than third place. We needed a miracle. And this kid was supposed to be just that: the next Babe Ruth, the next Ty Cobb, and yup, even the next Joe DiMaggio, all rolled into one!

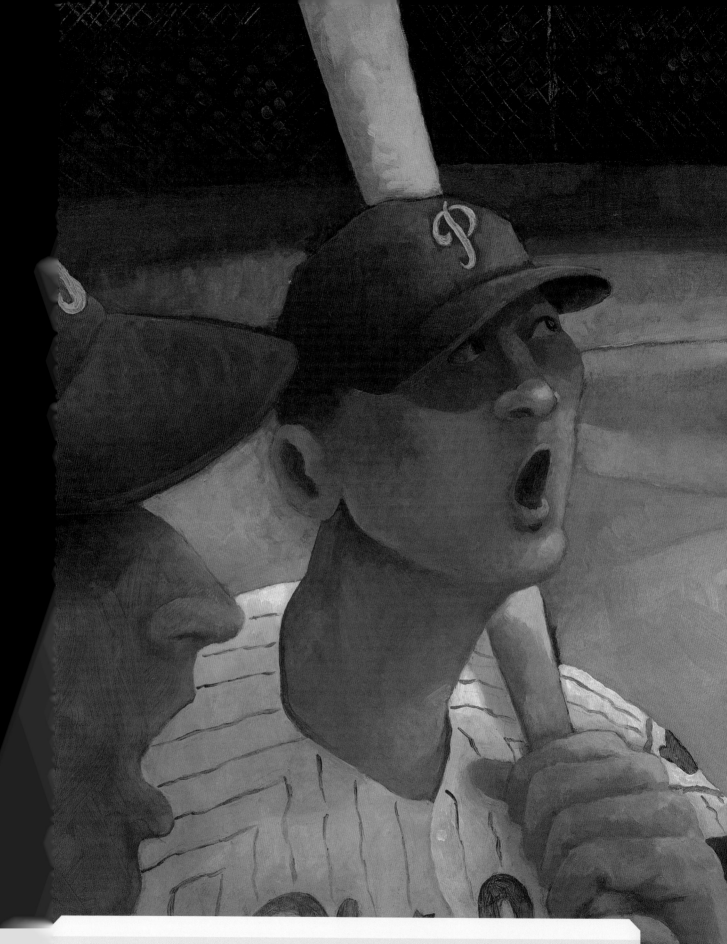

WILLIE MAYS'S FIRST SEASON: ROOKIE OF THE YEAR!

AT BATS	BATTING AVERAGE	HITS	HOME RUNS	FIELDING %	PUTOUTS
464	.274	127	20	.976	353

Long story short—Mays did not disappoint. Before his
first game as a Giant, in Philadelphia, Willie was takin' practice
cuts like guys do during warm-ups, and suddenly everyone, even the
Phillies, stopped what they were doin' and watched, jaws dropped, while
this young black guy walloped ball after ball over the fence—one to the left-field
grandstand, one off the scoreboard, one into the stratosphere. Well, they hadn't
seen NOTHIN' yet.

For instance, his first at bat at the Polo Grounds, the Giants' stadium,
up against Warren Spahn, one of the greatest pitchers of all time:

"Mays takes a curveball that just paints the outside corner for strike one.
Mays might be just a l-l-l-little overmatched right here. Next pitch—swung on
and missed. The count: 0 and 2. Here comes the pitch. . . .

"*Mays connects! That ball is headed for the—no, it CLEARS the LEFT-FIELD ROOF!!! Willie Mays, in his first at bat in New York, has sent one out of the stadium!*"

Silence falls over the stands. Then, like a tidal wave, comes this ROAR! A twenty-year-old rookie, a kid, had awakened the sleeping Giants. Geez, what a way to say "I'm here!"

BEST ALL-AROUND HITTERS IN MAJOR LEAGUE HISTORY

	AT BATS	BATTING AVERAGE	HITS	HOME RUNS	RBIS	STOLEN BASES	MVP
Babe Ruth	8,399	.342	2,873	714	2,213	123	1
Ted Williams	7,706	.344	2,654	521	1,839	24	2
Lou Gehrig	8,001	.340	2,721	493	1,995	102	2
Hank Aaron	12,364	.305	3,771	755	2,297*	240	1
Willie Mays	10,881	.302	3,283	660	1,903	338	2

*All-time record

And what he goes on to do that season—not just for the Giants, but for all of baseball—can't be explained with numbers or stats. It was how he went all out, every single moment, flyin' round the bases so fast that his hat would fly off, chargin' line drives hit to shallow center field like his life depended on it, usin' his classic "basket catch," his glove held out like he was askin' for a cookie, cool as he could be, and makin' throws no other human could make, includin' one so great it got nicknamed the Throw: *"Willie Mays . . . is reaching up with one hand, he's got it, he spins 180 degrees. Cox breaks for home. Wait a minute! Wait a minute! The ball comes into Westrum on the fly. Cox slides, and Westrum cuts him down at the plate! Cox is out! Billy Cox is out!"*

Catch, throw, run, hit, slug—Mays could do it all, and he could do it with *style*, my friend.

To us kids, Mays was just like a big kid himself. He was one of us, and we loved him. And he loved us right back. Talkin' to the fans, he'd always say "Hey!" in that high-pitched voice that earned him the nickname the Say Hey Kid.

But what we all loved best was how *hard* he played. Mays tried so hard he sometimes passed out right there on the field! They'd have to carry him off on a stretcher. And then, after games, he'd go back home to Harlem and play stickball on St. Nicholas Place with the neighborhood kids. It was like he couldn't stop! The Polo Grounds, the streets—he didn't care where he was playin'.

Then, like a lotta guys his age, Willie got
drafted by the army at the start of '52—and
had to spend two years in a uniform that didn't
say "Giants." By '53, the Giants had slid back
into fifth place. And us fans, we'd stopped goin'
to the games. What was the point?

Yep, we was all countin' the days till Willie
returned, and when he finally did, he no longer
looked like a kid. He's up to his fightin' weight
of 185—all of it solid muscle. But . . . can he
still play?

GREAT PLAYERS WHOSE CAREERS WERE INTERRUPTED BY MILITARY SERVICE
(AND WHOSE CAREER TOTALS ARE LOWER BECAUSE OF THIS)

	YEARS SERVED IN U.S. ARMED FORCES
Willie Mays	2
Joe DiMaggio	3
Ted Williams	5
Hank Greenberg	5
Bob Feller	4

Can he still *play*? Hah! Game One of the 1954 World Series. Giants and Indians. That's right, with Mays back, the Giants had made it to the Series—with the whole country watchin' on TV. Score's tied 2–2 in the eighth. Vic Wertz at bat for Cleveland. Two guys on, nobody out. With the count 1 and 2, Wertz SLAMS the ball to deep center field . . .

. . . and—BAM—Willie's runnin' like a madman . . . without even lookin'! This was crazy! I mean, this is a shot NO ONE catches—not even the Say Hey Kid. It was hit too far, too hard, and Willie *has his back to it*—lookin' like he might run smack into the WALL! Still, he keeps on barrelin', at one point doin' that thing he does when he knows he'll make the catch, tappin' his glove with his right fist. . . .

TWO OTHER LEGENDARY CATCHES

April 28, 1920, Chicago White Sox vs. Cleveland Indians: Indians center fielder Tris Speaker slammed into a wall to catch a line drive by Shoeless Joe Jackson. Though Speaker was knocked out, his glove remained tightly wrapped around the ball.

August 2, 1939, Detroit Tigers vs. New York Yankees: The Yankees' Joe DiMaggio ran 100 feet to catch a towering blast by Hank Greenberg. Graceful as ever, DiMaggio did NOT crash into the wall (but he came very close!).

"There's a long drive waaaaaaay back in center field, way back, waaaaaaaaaaay back—it is a . . . Oh, MY! . . . CAUGHT BY WILLIE MAYS!!! WILLIE MAYS just brought the crowd to its feet . . . with a catch . . . which must have been an optical illusion to a lot of people. BOY!"

BEST DEFENSIVE CENTER FIELDERS IN MAJOR LEAGUE HISTORY	CHANCES	PUTOUTS	ASSISTS	DOUBLE PLAYS	FIELDING %	ERRORS
Willie Mays	7,431	7,095*	195	60	.981	141
Tris Speaker	7,459	6,788	449*	139	.970	222
Ty Cobb	7,024	6,361	392	107	.961	271
Richie Ashburn	6,377	6,089	178	43	.983	110
Joe DiMaggio	4,774	4,516	153	30	.978	105

*All-time record

Willie twirls around and FIRES that ball to the infield, which keeps the runner from scoring and helps win the game! In this one play, he defies the Laws of Nature, Gravity, Baseball, Common Sense, Eyesight— and probably a few other laws too! Unbelievable!

You could fill a whole book with all the jaw-droppin' plays Willie made, all the homers he hit, all the bases he stole. But what made "the Catch" in '54 so special was that millions of people all over America had *seen* it on TV— it was the first time a lot of white folks had ever witnessed a black player who *really was* like Babe Ruth, Ty Cobb, and Joe DiMaggio all rolled into one. Heck, even Joe D. had to admit: Willie had the best arm that ever was.

Just look at him: Even as he falls to his knees after makin' that play, his eyes still takin' in the path of the ball—even then, you could see he was mentally still in the game, wantin' to win, never givin' up, ready for more.

Yessir, in that one moment when
Willie made the Catch, he showed the
world a new way of playing the game.
He changed how people saw his skin.
In his own way, he changed the world.

HIGHLIGHTS OF WILLIE MAYS'S CAREER (WITH RANKINGS ON ALL-TIME LEADERS LISTS)

	HOME RUNS	TOTAL BASES	RUNS	RBIS	HITS	PUTOUTS	GOLD GLOVES	ALL-STAR
Totals	660	6,066	2,062	1,903	3,283	7,095	12	24
Rankings	4th	3rd	7th	10th	11th	1st	1st	1st

Besides his Rookie of the Year Award, Willie Mays won two Most Valuable Player awards and is in the Major League Baseball Hall of Fame.

GLOSSARY OF BASEBALL TERMS

All-Star: A player who gets chosen for the annual All-Star Game, which takes place between two teams composed of the best players in the American League and the National League.

American League: One of two groups of teams in Major League Baseball.

Assist: The act of fielding a ball, then throwing it to another player covering one of the bases for an out.

At bat: A plate appearance in which a batter reaches base either through a hit or a fielding error—or is called out for any reason other than a sacrifice bunt or sacrifice fly. If the batter walks or is hit by a pitch, his plate appearance does not count as an at bat.

Batting average: Hits divided by at bats.

Chances: The total number of fielding opportunities for a player, composed of putouts, assists, and errors.

Double play: A play in which two players are put out.

Error: A fielding mistake that allows an opposing player to reach base.

Fielding percentage: The percentage of times a fielder successfully fields a ball—determined by dividing the total number of putouts and assists by the total chances.

Giants: One of the oldest National League teams—founded in 1883 and originally called the Gothams (until 1885). They played in New York until 1957 and then moved to San Francisco.

Gold Glove: An award given every year to the best fielders at each position; it was started in 1957.

Hit: When a batter makes contact with the ball using his bat and gets safely to one of the bases.

Home run: A hit in which the batter circles all four bases to score a run.

MVP (Most Valuable Player): An award given every year by the Baseball Writers' Association of America to the top player in both the National League and the American League.

National League: The older of the two groups of teams in Major League Baseball.

Putout: An out made by a fielder by catching a fly ball, tagging a runner or the base the runner is running to, or catching the third strike.

RBIs (runs batted in): Runs that score as the result of a player's at bat (even if the ball is caught or the player is tagged out), except in instances resulting from an error or a double play.

Total bases: The total number of bases a hitter reaches through his hits.

World Series: The best-of-seven championship series played by the National League and the American League pennant winners.

ABOUT THE STATISTICS IN THIS BOOK

Here are the online resources from which my statistics come:

baseball-almanac.com

baseballhalloffame.org

baseballlibrary.com

baseball-reference.com

coe.ksu.edu/nlbemuseum/history/
players.html
(Negro Leagues Baseball Museum eMuseum)

negroleaguebaseball.com

nlbpa.com (Negro League Baseball Players Association)

Baseball statistics have always been and will always be interpreted differently by different fans and scholars. Often, several fans will use the same set of statistics to come up with entirely different top-ten lists. This is a very subjective and sometimes sentimental process, not an exact science. And the arguments that inevitably arise are as much a part of the baseball tradition as peanuts and Cracker Jack.

A NOTE ABOUT THE RADIO BROADCAST QUOTES

Of the four excerpts from radio broadcasts (which are in italics), only the final two are actual quotes. These last two represented famous moments in baseball history—the first known as the Throw and the second known as the Catch—and in both instances I've preserved the announcer's words as they were in the transcript of the broadcast. For the first two broadcast moments (for which no transcript or audiotape exists), I've done my best to re-create what would likely have been broadcast over the radio at these points in history.

ABOUT THE AUTHOR AND ILLUSTRATOR

JONAH WINTER is an avid baseball fan and still has the baseball card collection he started as a kid. He is also the highly acclaimed author of many books for children, including *You Never Heard of Sandy Koufax?!*, which received three starred reviews and was named an ALA-ALSC Notable Children's Book and a *Booklist* Top of the List. His other books include *Here Comes the Garbage Barge!*, a *New York Times* Best Illustrated Book; *Barack*, a *New York Times* bestseller; *Dizzy*, the recipient of Best Book of the Year awards from *Booklist, School Library Journal, The Horn Book Magazine, The Bulletin of the Center for Children's Books*, and *Kirkus Reviews*; and *Roberto Clemente: Pride of the Pittsburgh Pirates*, an ALA-ALSC Notable Children's Book and a Bank Street College of Education Best Book of the Year.

TERRY WIDENER has had a lifelong interest in sports, both as a player and a fan. He collaborated with Jonah on one previous picture book, *Steel Town*. His other books for children include many award-winning baseball books, such as *Lou Gehrig: The Luckiest Man* by David A. Adler, a *Boston Globe–Horn Book* Honor Book, an ALA-ALSC Notable Children's Book, and an IRA Teachers' Choice; *The Babe & I*, also by David A. Adler, recipient of the California Young Reader Medal; and *Girl Wonder: A Baseball Story in Nine Innings* by Deborah Hopkinson, a *Parents' Choice* Gold Award Winner and a *Nick Jr. Family Magazine* Best Book of the Year.